# NIGHT LADDER

## WINNER OF THE 2017 BEST BOOK AWARD

POEMS BY

## LOIS P. JONES

GLASS LYRE PRESS

Cover art: "Bearer of Wonderment" © Andy Kehoe Art
Interior Photographs:
              p. iii:  Rilke's Bayon, photograph by Erica Schroeder
              p. 83: Susan Rogers
Design & layout: Steven Asmussen
Copyediting: Linda E. Kim

Glass Lyre Press, LLC
P.O. Box 2693
Glenview, IL 60025
www.GlassLyrePress.com

*To my sister Nancy, who gives*
*meaning to my life's purpose.*

## RILKE'S BAYON

When your roots, thick as the legs of a Dong Tao chicken
reached down into the earth. When your body
twisted up and took over the stones of a crumbling temple
in an attempt to survive. When the world wanted
to displace you. When the water made its journey
and did not return. When you knew your prayers
would only fall without ripening. Only then,
when the wind slashed your waist and you called out
to the stars. An answer. *In you, who were a child once – in you.*

# CONTENTS

## Two (cont'd)

## Three

## Four

# FIVE

# Acknowledgments

Grateful acknowledgment is extended to the following publications and/or organizations, in which some of the poems from this manuscript have appeared or are forthcoming:

*Poemeleon:* "Rilke's Bayon" and "Beyond Diagnosis"
*Tiferet:* "I Want to Know When," "Shema," and "Big Tujunga"
*American Poetry Journal:* "Unmarked Grave"
*Wide Awake:* Poets of Los Angeles anthology, Pacific Coast Poetry Series *(Beyond Baroque Books):* "Kensington Concierge"
*Poetry in the Windows 2014 Selection (Arroyo Arts Collective):* "Apple"
*Anne Frank Academy Permanent Exhibit:* "What the Chestnut Tree Saw"
*Pirene's Fountain:* "Alchemist," "In-Between Lives," "Late Winter"
*Arsenic Lobster:* "Birthday"
*Qarrtsiluni:* "Paris"
*Cruzio Café Animations:* "Picasso's Garden"
*One (Jacar Press):* "Rilke's Maid, After Wagner's Parsifal"
*Cultural Weekly:* "One" and "Red Horse"
*Warwick Review:* "Sastrugi"
*Sierra Nevada Review:* "In Full Bloom"
*Raven Chronicles:* "Ouija"
*Poetic Diversity:* "Self Portrait"
*Prism Review:* "Under a Mendoza Trellis"
*Tupelo Quarterly:* "Reading 'Shadowlands' to a Friend at the Sepulveda Dam"
*Cider Press Review:* "At Le Petit Pontoise Café"
*St. Julians Press:* "To the Moon on the Subject of Darkness"
*Poets on Site:* "How She Paints Herself"
*Eyewear Publishing (Poet's Quest for God Anthology):*
        "The Landscape of Flight"


*Bristol Poetry Prize*
"Foal"


*Bridport Poetry Prize*
*Shortlisted:* "Four Nights in the Misty Fjords"

*Tiferet Poetry Prize*
"The Scent of Ariel"

*Pirene's Fountain's Liakoura Prize*
"Demure"

*Web Del Sol:*
"Goose Step" judged by Fleda Brown
"Postcards to Samsara" judged by Robert Lee Brewer
"Ouija" judged by Fiona Sampson; also named Poem of the Year by
        *New Yorker* staff writer (2010)
"Ways to Paint a Woman" judged by Ruth Ellen Kocher
"Outside of the World" judged by Richard Krawiec
"Grand Canyon" judged by Kelly Cherry

# ONE

Perhaps the old monks were right when they tried to root love out; perhaps the poets are right when they try to water it. It is a blood-red flower, with the color of sin; but there is always the scent of a god about it.

—OLIVE SCHREINER

# ON THE SOUTHERN END OF CHARMOUTH ROAD

*for Lia, after reading Margo Berdeshevsky's*
*"Between Soul and Stone"*

No simple toll, these are Stedman bells
pealing around us like musical mortar,

scattering pigeons in the dove tower.
We came with the wandering

and the uphill pallor. Greened it up
toward a crackling blue, hair flying

like a lullaby, curling into oarweed
as we kept our ascension. We struck

the distance, calves full hard
as lamb bells. Our robes whipping

the sea. The wind soul is what
we're doing.  Still up, until the bells

were crying all around, no bones
to cradle them. Scaling the colonnade

of tombstones, chalcedonic and thin
as wafers.  We saw through them

to the graves below. The lambs
were buried there. Bleating through stone

heavier than a man, carried by hand
across the channel for monks like us.

Made by monks like us.

# Rilke's Maid, Leni at the Little Castle of Schloss Berg

*She is hardly there, she never asks me anything and never seems surprised at anything. She has a presence that is so to speak, climatic....*

— *Rilke*

I often see you like a monk looking out the manor windows
long after the last coals ember to ash. Ice seals the panes –

your quiet is soft as this fine snow falling outside
time. And when your eyes meet mine, I won't be drawn

into their storm, entering only to stoke the fire
or leave cheese and bread near your desk. You eat poorly

or not at all and sometimes I find you asleep, a book
face down in your lap – a hinged bird turned cold

in your hands. I do not wash her perfumed gloves
or tidy loose love letters near a torn slip

of words: *I am here, you will find me where you want me...*
Their blue reminds me of the rook thrush I freed

from your bedroom curtains. We live with little
sound, the only music in rain's benediction

or the odd chur of the nightjar. This evening's
new moon rises over the pine, your face riven

by its light as you enter your world
of shadows.  I will be the spirit of your

departed, aloft as a white moth in winter,
more cumulus than bone.

# UNMARKED GRAVE

*All I want is a single hand, A wounded hand if that is possible.*

— *Lorca*

Beautiful man, with your brows of broken ashes
and eyes that migrate in winter,

a hollow in your hand
where the moon fell through.

I could have kissed your mouth,
passed an olive with my tongue,
the aftertaste of canaries on our breath.

But the shriek of the little hour
is spent, and there is no road back.

The day it happened
there were no good boys
or dovecots filled with virgins,

just a sun imploding
like a sack of rotten oranges,

the scent of basil
from the grove near your home
and the piano that still waits for you.

No one will remember
the coward who shot you,
but the sheets,

the white sheets you sail on,
coming home.

# LATE WINTER

I like it when you're quiet.
The way your shadow fills me

with solitude.  With the face
of a red hibiscus

overturned into this stream.
The patience of a well worn

bench empty and expectant.
You don't need words

to coax a season.
To translate borealis, kisses

in the archway. The crinoline skirt
of the camellia that tricks you

into thinking it's a rose. Here
under this lintel of silence a river birch

shows only skin, pale as a prayer
and twice as lonely.

Around it, everything
in early bloom.

# KENSINGTON CONCIERGE

At 3:00 a.m. I'm wide open as the window.
The moon offers what little light it has
bringing London's ghosts – stray thoughts

of streetwalkers climb the flues,
and take root. This room holds its hurts –
swollen feet, bent neck, the width of the lift

when you looked in me. Some part of us rose
to the surface then silvered as it sank.
An odd pull, like a thread

in the underwing, but I kept
from touching your velvet yarmulke,
rubbed my voice for a path to speak.

I know you. You are dark oil
in a new lamp and even if you give your days
to the opening of doors

or the recovery of what we lost –
a red glove or a gentleman's cufflink,
my leather diary full of words of you

left on the clean sheets, you are still my keeper
of the lantern and there's only this pale hour
illumining your raven suit, its cotton so close

to my fingers. I've only had one tryst in my life,
but Levi I would break the rule for you –
break it like matzo on a candled night. I want

to hear you explain the strange razor calls
of rooftop birds, our vowels rain-lipped. You are
the kind of man who looks with your whole body.

Come here in your night coat like a Cossack.
Come in – your dark curls still, untouched.

# FOAL

*after reading "Fugue for Other Hands" by Joseph Fasano*

In your next life you will be
birthed in needles
of hoarfrost, your eyes still
in the blue gauze between

this world and the next
and I will kneel so close
you will smell the hot iron
waiting to singe

your skin.  You'll hear
the crackle of the flame
and your throat will prickle
with stars.  I'll wrap your shins

in nettle and this shelter will fall
deeply into zero. This is the start
of your suffering for the children,
*yours* who became

the wanderers, beaten between
the withers, broken and unridable
in the world's dark loam. There is
no animal to save you now

no purling stream to fold
shame into, not even the jackdaw
as witness, or a single crofter
awake in this cat's eye hour.

Revenge tries on its black
bridle then drapes it over
the swinging fence.
Father, I will not take out

your eyes but I will brand you
with the word you fear
and you will wear it
and you will wear it

and give up everything to winter.

# AFTERSTORM

These red hours –
    woodbine
        and winterberry,

red shouting
    like a woman
        too long quiet.

Snowbound, crabapple,
    pocked as a stone
        in the palm.

The last foliage
    fallen like one
        who keeps

no promise. Red
    of wet roofs
        of wood barns

and damp hay
    in a season
        without virgins.

# THE SCENT OF ARIEL

When the shuttle arrives at the old wooden doors,
her luggage bulging with too many dresses
and *gringa* lotions, books she won't have time to open,
when the teenage boy smiles after hauling the world

four flights of terra cotta steps to her room
with views of Calle Canal and red rooftops
clinging to early winter warmth, it won't be
the earthy scent of pink geraniums outside her window

or last night's wood smoke and kerosene
that fills her lungs, but the freshly washed shirt
of the boy, neat as his perfect teeth, the scent –
part lather, part lavender. She won't call it innocence,

though it comes close. Closer is the lack of artifice,
the way she tries to lose her paleness by slipping
into a red *robozo*, the comfort of towels laundered
in sunshine. And if this country is not hers,

if some resent her place here, still Ariana
remembers her each year and brings extra towels
that smell sweet as a tamale husk, rough as a night
of too many sangrias when bells

of the Parroquia jangle like cast iron pans,
and she believes every tourist is a burro
without a master, grazing on what it can,
pretending there is somewhere to belong.

# Two

Silently, God opens his golden eyes
over the place of skulls.

—GEORG TRAKL

# Apple

I am an apple in the pocket
of this old coat of yours, honest

and round. Feel me blindly
with rough hands.  Dare to take

me out and examine the deep wine
bruises, the garnet wounds.

What green is left reddens quickly
in your palm. Twist my stem

between your fingers until it snaps then
lay me down on the pine table.

Split me open with your sharpest knife.
Your tongue draws out each seed –

dark eyes that want to grow in you.
Place this slice between your lips.

One bite to remember an orchard.

# GOOSE STEP

*The Goose-Step... is one of the most horrible sights in the
world, far more terrifying than a dive-bomber.*
                                            —George Orwell


He loves to goose-step in her parking lot,
fluorescent light casting the stage
for Dachau.  Grins in his brown-skinned suit,
marveling at how the Germans treated him
like a countryman.  He admires the coarse
consonants, the wild sex with the Hamburg
girl he'd had on the road to Spain.

Sometimes he wanders through Jewish
graveyards feeling the faded dates
of tombs. Tells her the swastika's
Neolithic symbol appeared 10,000 years
before Christ. That stepping is a tradition
from the 17th century. How the Prussian army
stepped on the faces of their enemies.

She finds him aesthetic, like the tall leather boots
of the Reichswehr. Tries to think about the *duende*
in his flamenco guitar – the hollows of his voice
unbedding a demand. She prays the neighbors
are not looking and begs him to stop.  He smirks,
lifts his legs higher and higher.

# After Wagner's Parsifal

and the red silk sheets
    surge on stage like Moses'
        engorged sea

after the servants kneel and pray
    as King Amfortas is brought down
        on his bed to the forest lake

to bathe his wound
    after a mother in her scarlet dress
        lures the boy Parsifal to her side

we leave the theater's blackout
    of the senses
        silhouettes exit in spiked heels

and felt hats down the brass bannister
    toward flood lights and the scent
        of stale coffee and fine cigars

a man quotes Hitler in the hall
    *one can serve God only*
        *in the garb of the hero*

I think of the well-dressed Nazis
    who committed suicide
        at the end of the war

beyond the black doors of the opera house
    the city's sirens loose in us
        like a virulent disease

# WHAT THE CHESTNUT TREE SAW
# (AUGUST 4, 1944)

*The two of us looked out at the blue sky, the bare chestnut*
*tree glistening with dew ... and we were so moved and*
*entranced that we couldn't speak.*

*—Anne Frank*

A shape through the skylight—
pale knees crossed like driftwood.

Your face is a small bird,
hands darting in dips and starts
of a pink checkered book.  You track
the swoop and lunge of gulls
as flight lingers beneath your lids.

It's August and the window is open
for a breath of air.  Miner moths flutter
and spawn. Their brood transforms me
to late summer browning, a uniform of decay
I will flush back from. Tonight, only the moon

silvers your eyes as you lie in Peter's arms.
I watch canals stretch like felled trees, a city
quietly cut at the limbs. Then a day
that follows any other night.

A sun rises. A car halts and spills
its black-clotted men.  The last scampering
as you grab your twill coat, look up at me,
then away.

After the battle of rot, fifty years of fungus
and infested with moths, even the steel welds
they built could not prevent the gale storm
from snapping my neck.

A crane lifts me,
branches grazing the rooftop
the way a boy's knees touch a girl's.

What spring has done to us – white candleblooms
and their pale buds open, then burst.

# I Want to Know When

*for Tina*

my peach tree will bloom so I can lose
my mind in their fragrance.  Will they be white

or pink, Redhaven or Harmony?  And if it's true
all babies learn their mother's scent, will its flowers

hold the perfume of its fruit?  I want to know how
the yield will come, what I'll feel as the globes grow

and ripen beyond my door. How the fruit
will enter my dreams and I'll awaken,

shaken with longing. I want to bite
into its golden flesh to the red tinge that nests

the stone and see it burst like an ode—
to name its glistening taste, hook my hands

on my hips and drawl *hey mister, we've got the best peaches
west of Georgia.*  I want to feel the weight, its navel soft

as a baby's belly. To know how something so small
could yield so much and with all

my flowering, I did not bear fruit. And I will lie
down near its roots, stretched out among tansy

and marigolds, dusk-winged as a night pollinator
and dizzy above this rolling earth.

# DEMURE

She pours the cabernet
to show you its flame.
Your large hand lifts the glass

to examine love's color.
Isn't a stem sensual she thinks;
like Monet's *Poplars on the Epte.*

You wonder if this
is how she tastes –
dark and musky as earth.

Want to see her eyes dim
to red smoke, hear her voice
knot around yours in a husky tangle.

Thoughts quiver like moths.
It's hot so she snaps her fan
and the room opens into brocade.

Tonight, she's a dark episode.
Everywhere you touch burns.
How much heat will you believe?

# Birthday

Who knows the birth of a firecracker?
I hear they roasted bamboo to create a sound
loud enough to scare away ghosts. The rods sizzled
and blackened, then popped. At the end
of the Song Dynasty, the first manmade bursts – gunpowder
in a paper tube until they'd learned to string them

with hemp. Now they could hear them all at once –
the hundred-break crackers crackling in the night,
exciting a burn in the heart's moist chamber.
I was too young for explosions. For me,
there was only longing, a sparkler in the dark,
a flare built to last a moment. My small arm

spinning a circle of light, a golden diadem I could wear
like a fairy princess.  How could I know dreams escape
as alchemy? That time is not trapped beneath
a crystal dome but a night of humid air, the black snake's
smoke and hiss as it curls out of the tablet,
flares into a pharaoh's serpent as we watch charmed

in the alley. My sister kneels on cement, snapping the paper
roll caps with a sharp rock, our noses stung with sulfur.
We are rockets fired from a glass Coke bottle, the pyrotechnic
possibility of flight. It is an hour, a joy of country
being born. A belief that beginnings made everything possible,
like life in a mother's womb.

And I thought it was all for me, born on a day when the night
splinters, aflame in wonder,
unconcerned with what occupies the dark.

# PARIS

*after Johannes Bobrowksi's "Fishingport"*

At evening, as snowflakes fall
one after the other,
then I love you.

I love you in the uncomfortable bed,
on the second floor of the converted horse barn
in the shadow of a new moon
on the sheet's iron warmth.

Our mouths are tricked with licorice —
you come, unconcerned with Henri's key.
The Eiffel has stopped glittering
and the man who raged at his wife
has left the metro long ago.

Here you come with your sweet mouth.
Now you walk across the last snow.

# Picasso's Garden

*for Dora Maar*

He tears from my skin like a necessary thorn,
directs which way my limbs will bend;

how pungent the scent of each blossom.
Plants me next to hollyhocks and winged seeds

of pine, places his paint brush in the tomato can,
demands I grow near wisteria. I witness her shells

in the breeze; how she dabs the perfume of mauve water
between her legs, offers him the sympathy

of a dandelion. In spring, a peony tempts him
with her red fist. He will part her like a cheap carnation

and there's nothing I can do about it. I was born with a nub
that will not open, a womb blank as a canvas. He says

we all must sacrifice, but I stop giving it away, shut down
my nectar and bury its scent. He swallows me anyway,

like thistles of burdock, makes me believe
he loves my bitterness. I endure the scent of peat on his lips,

pack his brushes and pretend he is leaving, but we carry
one another's seed. He will chase me into the afterlife.

Here is the profile I must not sketch—hornets humming
along the edge of his jaw.

# ONE

One lifetime she drank water from his skull.
She gilded the bones with gold and struck them
in the dirt.   She pounced a vowel that was her name.
But now she is no one.  She has the privilege
of ambiguity.  Being one white woman,
being from nowhere but earth
and a father who lost his mind
in the metal.

Being this way, she is; an American
indistinguishable as a flesh tree
in the desert.  She wishes for a name
like Kandinsky, Levertov.  How about Stradivarius?
How about dinner on the 41st floor?  She did arrange this.
She did write the composer a letter.

*Meet me on the roof of One Wilshire.*

She brought wine and a white summer
dress.   She brought nothing underneath
but the long boulevard of empty offices
lit up like an afterthought.   The cot
she carried up 11 flights of stairs.  She brought
the night, slippery as a man on wheels.
She wheeled the stars until they were all
in their right places.  She gave him all
the words an evening has for loneliness.

# THREE

"You listen to people, you listen so deeply that you can hear their past lives, The crackle of their funeral pyres."

—DICK ALLEN

# FOUR NIGHTS IN THE MISTY FJORDS

She was inside the whalebone
counting the looped ritual
that followed her below deck.
She was the smell of crayfish
and crab, cracking them open,
tearing out their sweet meat.
This is what she did when the shells
split. She kept them until they dried
inside like a gull's white dung.
She layered the hours with it –
when everyone lay in their bunks
and the stars were hammers on the sea.
She could feel their weight – hear
the surrender of the old halibut
before the hook found passage.
Blackwater pulling on a line,
pulling like the night, creaking
like a lie. And when she closed her eyes
and her body sank down
that's when he would appear, cinch
in his hand, twisting the anchor
until it snapped, watching her drop
in the dark. The rope unravelling
from the rust so swiftly, it burned
to touch.  Nothing but nightfall
at the river's mouth and the slow
motion of salmon waiting to be caught.

# LAZARUS

*for G.W.*

There is no rising for you.
Not four days, not four months,
not forty years on ddd and zzz

and all of a medicated womb
from which no mother bore you.
I can smell you in the white halls

before I turn the corner. Urine
in the mind's brine without a mop
for your mess. You ask questions

and questions, your fists cycling
like a blind boxer in the direction
of my voice. And you, and you!

beating the air while my heart flees,
a goldfinch unable to land.
Am I standing? Yes, you are standing.

At 6'2" a pylon towering over
the nurses and me. Wondering whether
your heart still pumps or how time

turned in on itself like your toenails
curled into mollusks. I watch your eyes
roll up in a wave, bind into a clay

you cannot leave. Each night I shape
your body, push the solid form into hollow
until the whole of you opens – a jug I fill

with clear water. Drink no more
this earth my brother. Evaporate.
There's your answer.

# DEAR KALEIDOSCOPE

*for Leslie*

It's been years since childhood,
but every fractal still catches the sun,
turns its crystal gears like a factory

of light. Sapphire and ruby,
celadon and indigo –
I keep watching, mesmerized

by the sheer improbability
of repetition. Like you I spin
in a strange chamber of mirrors;

mandala to snowflake,
camellia to dwarf star,
shape shifting as if all lives pass

through an endless diadem of fire.
Keep looking, you said and I do,
for what are we given

in this human world but a few
beads to rattle
in a paper scope. I want to tell you

the world is still beautiful. Leaves
continue their graceful gavotte
falling into color as they tumble.

There are days to watch clouds
turn from oblivion into spectacle,
burning the world as they go.

# POSTCARDS TO SAMSARA

1.

he kept painting the planets
formed the moon from a ball of wax
hung it without a wick
positioned a star with enough distance
into the past it reached the future

2.

this glow which died light years ago
finds him the way a mirror reflects
from a wreck
at the bottom of an ocean

death draws a map
he must follow

3.

he kneels on the red woven mat
to balance perspective
while one hand tips
a brush to canvas

the dish of dark water
keeps a galaxy within time
his journal in search of a voice
a bonsai tree whose shadow
is an inkwell

4.

Perhaps Eve loved Adam
so much she gave away
all her memories
as if ignorance were a flood
a way to drown the animal
there are no flaming swords
guarding the gate
there's only me
trying to uncover our Eden
after all
I asked to be hungry
you consented to be tasted

# OUIJA

*"Green sunflowers trembled in the highlands of dusk and
the whole cemetery began to complain with cardboard
mouths and dry rags."*

— *Lorca*

You asked for an R, the ripening of olives
in your garden, a red-tailed hawk

angling over the road, the path
that took you down and away

from the empty room of the body.
The R of reasons, of the ringing that breaks

in a yellow bell tower – the only sound
after the round of shots that shattered

an afternoon. And the T can only be more time,
time to be the clock or the weather vane,

the twilight through your windows
on the page, your pen once again plow

and the places you took me
where I abandoned faith.

A is alone, how you never wanted it,
preferring the company of bishop's

weed and drowsy horses – the warm trace
of the lily and a flame,

for the Andalusian night and its black mouth
that sings your *saeta*. G is the ghost bird

hovering at Fuente Grande you did not
wish to come, for the grave some say

you dug with your own hands, empty
as a mouth of snow,

as a sky that held no moon that night,
only the names of the dead.

# UNDER A MENDOZA TRELLIS

Everything flows through me, but nothing
is lost, not a drop of wine or a breath

of rosemary. Across the pine table
you pour yourself like sun storm

on a thirsty riverbed, speak as if you know
the meaning of my name. You ask me

to bear this, to remember the scent of apples
and the green heart of the poplar growing

in endless rows. A woman is strumming guitar,
you are shirtless, wearing your curls

like a fever. The intricate pattern
of shadow under trellis. How you laugh

easily and deep, look straight into
my blood and I am as full as the grapes

in the canopy. Here is the impulse, strong
as the pull of strings. I try to lose you

in the gaucho's ballad, let the guitar soften time
in our bones. You spill another river of wine

in my glass, shake your head and smile
at my refusal. Your voice, smoke

of the *asado*. Today is a glass half drunk, a moment
of knowing how you pour, how you pour.

# Night Ladder (Milonga for a Blind Man)

*Time is both loss and memory.*
    —Borges

In the middle of the night
a blind man takes a key
from his pocket.

In the middle of the night
he climbs to the top of the stairs.
From his balcony he remembers daylight,

the crumbled cement and the cracks
on the tavern below. The way the sky spoke
to him, the last with anything to say.

And the opening of the flowers
when they would open for him.
Pink or coral, her lips staining his

with a memory – a breath
and a daydream of pampas
and hibiscus. His shirt unbuttoned

to the waist and the white skin
of a butterfly.  In the middle
of the night he remembers

a snow heart and the red walls
of morning.  How he walked the streets
in search of distance. Someone

has counted his days.  And this blindness
that followed, plucked out his eyes.
It always comes to this –

edges fading from the familiar,
a city vague and celestial. He has lost
count of all his endings.

# SASTRUGI

this is the hour
snow sifts across the tundra

blows in gusts that erode
the way only winter can

a soliloquy
where sound is absence

an imprint that hardens
to evidence

the way waves of white
crest and fix into feather

as if the land knows time
is a migrating bird

a perpetual flight
of arctic bodies

death as the invisible accomplice
to summer

a white deer returning
from the distance

cloaked in rain
and heavy light

who walks a long way
for a taste of salt

# FOUR

This world is my twin
but I was not cut from the same cloth, I passed
through the shadow so I could be
amazed at it.

—BRENDA HILLMAN - "THE SPELL"

# Reading "Shadowlands" to a Friend at The Sepulveda Dam

*for Russell*

*Did my eyes avoid yours, Brother?*
                                        *— Johannes Bobrowski*


Mustard grass to our hips – sallow as Gauguin's
Yellow Christ, it blows its seed, mixing

with the must of mule fat and sage. When the wind
is this strong, I remember the year branches twisted

from their trunks onto my path toward Terezin.
They were everywhere, needling the numbered

graves.  Anonymity makes war possible, otherwise
you couldn't look your brother in the eye—

become a slavering wolf, the SS who drove
the Jews toward the wild smell

in the woods and the old house
running down to the water. And you know

what's coming.  Listening as if you are a part
of the descent – the river and its copper-

colored trail – the blood wall where nothing
is wet only driven in like nails. It tastes of rust

in our mouths, of shadowlands and a boot
in the snow and even in this dry heat

your cheeks are damp. You know what a home
looks like because you came from a land

of sheepherders and milk cows, where ovens
were meant to keep a back warm in winter

and wagons bore the day's wheat.
What can we carry but a chance

to remember how a man is a lantern
lowered into the earth.

# AT LE PETIT PONTOISE CAFÉ

No other sky could hold such light,
not this afternoon outside Notre Dame

where the glow casts all of Paris
in Rodin's marble studio. A woman

slips past my window
as I sip the creamy surface

of my *café au lait* that mingles
with the apple's breath of tarte tartin.

Her skin a cool shale of cheek bones
and its history of crowns.  A poppy

for her lips above the pointed chin.
And her hair, dark as a Montmartre

night.  The taste lingered
in my bones.  Not lust but a memory

of light, the delicate walk that holds
a city in the body.  And everything

she passes moving through
the *rue* of her legs.

# AURORA BOREALIS

There's no separating your light from its source—
no unraveling neutrons that excite you to luminosity.

You are visible in the blackest fraction that circles
the ends of each pole, an incandescent shroud

to wash over me. Here, while the passengers' dreams
levitate over Greenland, I open the shade

to find you. The shock of an angel manifest in fire.
A shimmering hijab across the face of a woman. Desire

transmutes into an undulating surf and my wish
to keep you from going away. Only now can I recall

the way my breathing slowed to the rhythm
of your wave. My face aglow as if a dream

had visited. I wanted to shout, to shake every traveler
awake. No one can see you but me. This proof

dragging its white hem along a black beach. I know
who you are. Abandoned light,

now found, now lost. Nothing to keep
as evidence.

# Red Horse

No one understood this blood run
to the moon, this blaze

of you, red horse in a swollen sky.
How you turned loose

like a fistful of fire ants.
How your temper could burn

a field when there was too much
to drink. There were days we'd spread

the blanket on the grasses
near the sycamores and let the desert

air run through us,
let the sage burn our nostrils

as we sipped a silky *rioja*.
A wine you liked to translate,

as you decoded everything beautiful.
Your lips full and slightly curled

*siempre, siempre: jardin de mi agonia,*
*tu cuerpo fugitivo para siempre,*

*always, always: garden of my last breath,*
*your body escaped forever,*

Lorca in his red shoes
lighting our tongues, lifting

our hips until the sun
turned poppy and burst.

# Ways to Paint a Woman

*after a portrait by Ali-Al Ameri*

Sometimes only color can speak
for the heart.

Sometimes you must paint it yellow—
listen with the eyes: honeycomb and maize,

golden rainflowers.
Transform with your softest brush

the way Lorca's bathing girl liquefies
into water – half a head in fire,

sun burning a trail from forehead to cheek.
Graze the mouth with mango. Make time to blend

and take away. Use the green of a blind man
when he says *you're beautiful*

and means *you're timeless.*
Show what the light gave her

washing warmth into a neck
until it's dune, a cliffside

that holds a head of surf.
Paint as you would before you awaken,

when sunlight falls like milkweed
and you are an empty silo

letting her grain fill you –
buttery malt and biscuit

for the love of honey

# ALCHEMIST

*Inspired by the photograph "Birth of the Magi"*
*by Peter Shefler*


Magi, magos, maguš,
they say you were born

in a letting-go moment
when a Father knew

they needed more than magic.
When they could no longer gather

enough for the fire, you came,
an arrow of light

shot down from silence
to the great noise.

What did the nameless ones
hear who kept vigil

as a mother pushed
your skull from the void?

Her shrieks far
from the crowded kataluma

from the shepherds
and their flocks. The musk

of afterbirth still mingling
with the hot death

of lamb and ewe, the soft wool
of swaddling clothes

as they placed you
in the wooden trough.

Here you lie in a meadow
of nightfall, glowing like a child

who does not know his future.
Let me hold you,

your holy gold; all that pours
transforms.

# In Full Bloom

*After the photograph "Mostly Magnolia" by Peter Shefler*

You have made her
mostly magnolia.

As if a tree could rise
from nothing

but a glance. That's how
it goes. The clear night

has left its awakening
floating on the ridge,

petals opening to this one
thought. No, not opening,

slipping from a shoulder
like a pale chemise. You have

made her mostly magnolia –
pressed as sleep

in a thousand pages.
Time is a skyward thing,

but butterflies
ask no questions.

In their short life
they have flown

their destinies.  She will be
this perfection

painted into softness.
It's how you made her:

the breath and the scent
of things impossible to keep.

# GRAND CANYON, NORTH RIM

At the edge of a known world
mountains repeat themselves
like old people, each a blue syllable,
a language of forgetting.
A place like this, exposed
to harsh winters and long years
of drought begs to be left
as it was. One can't help
but be philosophical
standing at the chasm
above the seep willow
and the ghost water that once
raged like bison through the bottom
of this immense gorge. Not
from flash floods and snow melt
but a force so powerful
the ground split itself open
shearing the canyon raw.
What power could carry boulders
miles away?  Surely no slow,
methodical erosion but something
catastrophic, leaving this maw to gawk.
My tongue heavy now with dust
like a potter's wheel in the sun.
Nearly dusk and the red rock face
shifts mood, deepening with itself.
At last I am a shadow, a human sundial
at a precipice.  This gnomon slightly tilted
toward a true celestial north.

# SHEMA

*Listen!* the Rabbi says, God is One. *Listen for what comes next.*
*When death arrives shema is a mezuzah on the threshold*

of your lives, the soul's last words before leaving a body
but I hear only the rabbi's voice, this stranger

who entered the last ten minutes of a life
when your daughters and all their hours

could not give the word to let you go. A woman
who spoke past tubes and sheets, beyond a face

swollen from the fall and eyelids sealed
past opening. She told you what a good job

you'd done, forgave all the secrets – the locked
drawers finally open – their invisible contents drifting

in the clinical air. Her words were blood moving
through us as we held hands – the road and the river

as we felt you pass, not so heavy as a song,
not even snow on the bough melting.

# SPLENDOR

*Sunlight fell upon the wall; the wall received a borrowed splendor. Why set your heart on a piece of earth, O simple one?*

~ *Rumi*

1.

You are uncountable –
the single eye of a sunflower.

    The star-nosed mole
        whose fleshly face sprouts
                from the marsh or the collision
                        of the Cygnus cluster
                                in a cosmic swarm.

You are the jellyfish
at the bed of the Black Sea
or a coastline of phosphorous
beings along the Miles River.

    A woman who hears the call
        of the muezzin from the top
                of a Cairo roof or a mosque
                      of men with their backs to the sky.

2.

How sunlight flames the fig leaves each fall—
the tree she planted when father died.
Lawn chairs appear like apparitions
around its trunk as if someone wants
to catch its nuance from every angle,
as if the tree's eye had no boundaries.

3.

What illumines this footnote
to honey.  What did I do to destroy
its future when the bee flew low
and silent over my wood floors?
I could have scooped it in a jar
and set it free to die in the dove weeds.
I could have whisked it
out with my broom, but I threw my rug
over it and danced.  Drunk on the drizzle
of fear.  I confess to you my destruction.

4.

What the photographer captured
when she slipped the lens
inside the cello to reveal
the prayer that burns inside
every instrument
and you stood in its teak room
awash in the cleft of light
reserved only for the echoing notes
of Bach's holy chamber.

# SELF PORTRAIT

they say the right is the eye
of the father
it hides beneath a mantle
of low clouds
only the left asks if we see its seeing
do we sense what aquafies
even as the photograph closes
in on itself     everything around it
turned to black and white
the chiaroscuro it lives in
oceanic iris encircling
the pupil's *isla negra*
and its intake of breath
it is already forgetting
who it was
it is catching the last coin
of light as the dove coos
into the evening
something like a prayer

# FIVE

I do not think that I will touch the sky with my two arms.

—SAPPHO

# Reflections on La Scapigliata (The Girl With Disheveled Hair) by Leonardo Da Vinci

1.

this face, a house of stars before the fall
Lorca's *round silence of night*
*one note on the stave*
*of the infinite*
as if the head were a hermeneutic circle
that we may know the whole through our parts
the distance from chin to nose
and roots to eyebrows
in each    the same

you can feel Leonardo's brush above
the soft triangle of cheek
the light left below the eyes
rooms he admires but never enters

who knows what they have witnessed
pupils of a black moon
carry the codices of more
than one life
her thoughts cast toward
a world of inner frescoes

here is the spirit's underpainting
awash in a clear glaze
before a commitment to color
and don't think she is unaware
of her inner nudity        not as one would be
conscious of a body but the way a bolt
of silk rests
on the edge of a dune

2.

She can't stop looking in your direction. A horizon that never makes its way toward her. Her face as a field, hatch-marks of hay. Hair drawn from wild grasses. When daylight fell into this small room of her, the body seemed remote. There is a falling of hands, the light through the window making shapes until you leave.

3.

If she stepped out of her face just once
the landscape would be white foxes
at twilight.  Her hand
a frozen river, her mouth a creature
half locked in ice.  When she looks
at you without eyes you see your history
like the back of your head
winter is the god she returns to.

4.

disheveled
undone,
dis arrayed
let down,

the howl of human utterances
the hair
*à part de ça*

just as she is
just as I was
fresh from the ochre linens
feet padding on worn wood
leaving sunlight striped across the pillow

once I dreamed I awoke
in her body
it was me looking out
from the petite form
just the suggestion
of a swell below the neckline
like two koi coming up for air
I placed my palms on each gesture
this is what the mirror saw

# WHAT DRESSES YOU EACH DAY IN HARDWOOD

It is October, the season for hunting.
Something has entered the grove—

your mother's stern form as birch.
She is thin from frowning. She has born

the mark of your brother on her bark.
You can no longer regard her image

or look into its warnings. Even though you tried
to free him from a winter that sliced

his hooves. You took his hand when the arrow
breached skin and calmed

his eyes. There were years when the wind
awakened him with the applause

of dead leaves. Now you wonder whether
he will stand again. He has returned to the crepuscule

you will not enter. Outside, you are a sleepwalker
that knows her way to the cellar

door. Your mother is the birch that follows,
rising quickly no matter where you are. Even

as you leave the smell of hospital ammonia to hoarfrost.
Even this cold cannot keep her roots from catching

place. What will you do now that no hour
is clear felled and she has merged with the soil?

Soon the moss will grow. Soon her eyes will cover
with lichen and there will be birches in every room.

# QI (氣)

*Too much fire,*
he said. Close your eyes

and let
your illness ink the stream.

Abandon the wasp's sting
in winter. What you lost –

          tumbleweed.

When the river hits
the far side

of your house    wet
                 your wings.

# Beyond Diagnosis

*Lie down. Lie down and let the body become the promise*
*of no other.*

—Joseph Fasano

You sit by the river and watch your shadow
cross the grove of oaks away from you.
The moon dappling you into someone
you no longer know. Like the simple cell
multiplied        like rain        like mercury.
The silver of your fall into its unstoppable
creation. Your hands heavy with pails
of moonlight; a white fire you fling into the night
for an answer.  How you wondered why this eclipse
came to you and whether you will continue
or if even now some dark bird is repeating
in you its malignant fugue.

You've been carrying a body so long.  Sometimes
you want to lose it like a dark country
even though you'll have to return.  Even though
some memory will ice and crack its way back
to you.  No one could look at infinity
all at once, just as there is no one to hear
every prayer, but there is a presence who watches
and grows near you like a Bloodgood,
stout and florid faced.

God is the stranger you want to hold in your arms.
Your desire for solitude a delicious fruit.  Maybe you need
an entire lifetime without a body to consider the word *open*
or the phrase *it is late for blessings.* You could be carried
without form.  The way wind urges tumbleweed. How
it works in you like a thirst to touch the living, to kneel
like these camellia branches until you are lowered
into the river, your flowered face pushing past
its reflection. Death is the razor call of the crow
in these scrub oaks. Then the wind, if you are lucky,
and its forgiving song.

# TO THE MOON ON THE SUBJECT OF DARKNESS

*If anyone ever addressed you, it was with a breathless*
*"where are you going?"*

        *—Rilke*


I have been waiting
   and now you appear
between the yew's branches

luminous as a man
   who has seen the edge
of the universe. I've missed you

and asked questions
   of everything white:
frost birch and fog,

an egret feather that fell
   into the palm, even snow's
possibility of rumor,

but night moved
   to the riverbed
and stood nude and mute

in its shadow.
   The last time I saw you,
you were waning gibbous,

floating east as a daydream
   in blue.
The sky, like me, emptied too,

but for a few stars
   who dared to tell
you were the same moon

who made a mirror
        of yourself in the white
petaled Rowan, who sheltered

the poet as he slept
        in the cradle
of the Sphinx. The one

who lit Buddha's face
        as he realized nothing
is ever lost

in the universe.  Like Orion
        I have learned to wait. I let go
this belt of stars.

# BIG TUJUNGA
### for Alice

The wind is humming in your red dress.
The wind is humming in your red dress
*and the moon and stars do their slow*
*tambourine dance to praise this universe,* so Rumi says.
There is a glory in the way you stand

as if the body wants to move in quick arpeggio –
bouncing on a soul spring, letting the ground
raise you, breeze lifting your skirt as you walk
the wash and let your mind tango with creosote
and mesquite. This is where the Tongva slept

in huts made of willow and tule reed.  Right here
at the edge of the creek where families feasted
on acorns, cooked quail and rabbit
on soft ground near your roots.   Anything
could appear to you now—

ghost moths fluttering in the shadows,
ravens startling the jack rabbits
in the deer weed and sumac. Some spirit
rushing past you like tumbleweed.
The sun is staking its claim, turning your skin

to gold leaf. Time makes you thirsty,
hungry for what really feeds you.
You're hoping the bees will show
will hum you with their clear wings
will honey you and take you home.

# In Between Lives

She lets herself be known slowly,
illuminates rooftops in slants of ochre,
bathes the morning beasts, even

as the crow repeats its darkness.
Distinguishes her shadow by the quality
of light. The way yellow and blue tiles

are polished with early hours.
How she angles the shade
to soften the courtyard, the hush

of the fountain in a silvered museum.
A pigeon pauses on its bottom tier, falls asleep
in a pool of her warmth. She drifts

on to the next village, lingers over fruit stands
and laundry lines. Mountains return
from where they wandered in the night.

Here is her new mother; chestnut hair
tossed back in a blue ribbon,
belly swollen beneath

a linen shift. This will be her tiny
body. She can already smell the salty
air of the Black Sea.

# Outside of the World

Suppose the rain fell and only one man saw its fate.
Suppose the fate lay down and let the snow ice itself
and the world found a place for the next god

by the very nature of things, by the way the peach tree
takes on the sun even when it doesn't need it. The way
it holds it in its branches waiting for the moment

when a fruit will call it to its next life. Suppose the bird
that sits alone on the branch or the chair facing it
were the rain and the way it goes. Suppose the way

it goes was all a god could muster in a single hand
and that was the life he left you. Suppose you never leave
because arrival and departure

are a limp arm on an operating table, and when you left
the room you are still there with your secrets exposed.
Suppose a doctor is a preacher

with a knife and you have let your feathers fall
in a pattern of despair. Suppose this is the only way
you can live when your brother sits in a chair of iron.

Suppose he never really left you and the day began
with this wind in the branches and never ends.
Suppose your fingers were the flame of a life

you were still living. Suppose the man you wanted
came to you as if you were a house that was built
just for sleeping. Suppose your house caught fire

and that you lived this way because it's the only way
you knew.  Suppose the world kept spinning
on its white stem without need for plucking.

Even when it glistened like a ripe fruit
and all you could do was come back
and try again to taste it.

# HOW SHE PAINTS HERSELF

*after Susan Dobay's painting "Awakening"*
*inspired by Mary Kay Rummel*


Sometimes the yearning
burns so fiercely
it illumines a body

worthy of Gnostic devotion.
Better to paint one's self
from the inside out

better to believe in the light
that limns the brush.
Faith is in your hand—

in the way you reveal yourself
as an autumnal river,
dark moss jewelling

your inner thighs, flesh
fully exposed, sprawled
so comfortably below

the surface of things. Sunlight
kindles your waist,
defines your belly

as a golden island, a future
without need of horizon.
And your smile, satisfied

the way a woman knows
how to please herself
You lie back, elbows up,

welcoming the world
as lover. You were never
really a virgin.

Every part of you
meant to be known
born to say yes.

# THE LANDSCAPE OF FLIGHT

*for Susan Rogers*

> *Once you have tasted flight you will walk the earth with
> your eyes turned skywards, for there you have been and
> there you will long to return.*
>
> —Leonardo da Vinci

*1. Bone*

They say a hawk landed in your cradle
and swept its tail feathers past your mouth,
awakening a taste for flight,

your need to pull the buzzard apart
with slender fingers looking for secrets
in articulated wings. Here

in the late hours, the scent of wax burns
your nostrils as you pry the codex,
cracking the contours, drawing

the downy tufts in two. You note
the breast bone shaped like a keel,
lay out each pearled shaft

until it reclaims its shape. Candles come
and go like sylphs, casting shadows
on the freshly inked sketches. When you finally

walk the corridor to your room,
feathers fall to the tiled floors, lodge
in your velvet robes and pillows.
Sleep arrives
        slender as a wing bone.    You dream you are

a black crane flying low across the Arno,
                              the moon a plume nearly gone.


*2. Earth*

I've been trying for so long
to leave you, but gravity
pulls me back.

Maybe my wings
are too solid,
my breath heavy as salt,

bones too dense for the folds
of space where nothing
answers my call.


*3. Flower*

Look at these dogwood blossoms
caught in the act of flying,

white wings bent and touching
in a flock of origami.

They could be cranes adrift
in the impermanence of dying.

# NOTES

**Ariel** is the name of a laundry detergent available in Mexico.

An **asado** is the preparation and practice of cutting and grilling meat. A mainstay of Argentine culture, it goes far back in the country's history when gauchos roamed the pastures and cooked their dinners on makeshift grills and open flames.

The poem "Picasso's Garden" was inspired in part by Picasso's 1938 portrait of **Dora Maar,** *Seated Woman in a Garden.* In 1936 54-year old Picasso met Yugoslavian Dora Maar (1907 -1997), the photographer who documented Picasso's painting of Guernica, the 1937 painting of Picasso's depiction of the German's having bombed the Basque city of Guernica, Spain during the Spanish Civil War. A painter herself, she became Picasso's constant companion and lover from 1936 through April 1944. In later years she became a recluse, dying poor and alone.

**Duende** or *tener duende* ("having duende") loosely means having soul, a heightened state of emotion, expression and authenticity, often connected with flamenco. The artistic and especially musical term was derived from the duende, an elf or goblin-like Magic creature in Spanish mythology. Federico García Lorca first developed the aesthetics of Duende in a lecture he gave in Buenos Aires in 1933, "Juego y teoria del duende" ("Play and Theory of the Duende").

**Kataluma** — an inn, lodging-place.

The **Reichswehr** (English: Empire Defense) formed the military organization of Germany from 1919 until 1935, when it was united with the newly founded Wehrmacht ("Defense Force").

**Robozo** is a traditional Mexican shawl that is long enough to wrap around a woman's body.

**Saeta** is a revered form of Spanish religious song, whose form and style has evolved over many centuries. Saetas evoke strong emotion and are sung most often during public processions.

**Sastrugi** is a Russian word defined as a wind-eroded, hard-packed snow surface with irregular grooves and sharp ridges that is mostly found in the earth's polar regions as well as on mountains subject to high winds.

**Stedman Caters** refers to Fabian Stedman (fl. 1670).] In campanology, it is used to designate a method of bell ringing devised by Stedman. Stedman caters, Stedman cinques, Stedman triples.

See: https://www.youtube.com/watch?v=4rTnNedPHBU

\* "A man is a lantern lowered into the earth" is a paraphrase of something I read long ago. I cannot attribute its source but wish to acknowledge it here.

# Special Thanks

I'd like to express my gratitude to those poets who lit the path – Rainer Maria Rilke, Federico Garcia Lorca, Pablo Neruda and Paul Eluard. Later, it was my friend and first mentor Russell Salamon who encouraged and critiqued and continued to point toward the stars. Without his initial guidance (and Hafez-boot-kicking nature), I would not have found the door.

I must thank Peter Ludwin, a poet of exquisite gifts who brought me to the life-changing experience of San Miguel Poetry Week in 2005 and the subsequent five years I attended and for all the great faculty and friendships. To my dear friend across the pond, Lia Brooks who has been and continues to be a source of brilliance and inspiration ever since we connected in an on-line workshop some years ago.

Of the many who have helped over the past nine years – Susan Rogers, a poet of great spirit and musicality who is a member of both Westside Women Writers and Faraway Poets has been an enduring source of friendship and encouragement. More thanks to all the Westside Women Writers, Millicent Accardi, Maja Trochimczyk, Madeleine Butcher, Georgia Jones-Davis, Sonya Sabanac and Kathi Stafford as well as Kathabela Wilson, leader of Poets on Site, for her generosity and heart and the other Poets on Site members who've helped along the way. Thanks to the profoundly ecstatic Melissa Studdard who is a source of endless support and friendship and an aesthetic astonishment in my life.

The initial draft of this manuscript was shaped in 2012 in Languedoc, France with the help of Pascale Petit, a poet whose work I've long admired. Later, I spent time revising with Suzanne Lummis, who taught me about concision, clarity and elegance in the line and lent her own in support of this collection. Thanks to Katie Kingston and Allen Braden whose initial review and encouragement of the manuscript helped me to move forward and to April Ossman whose depth of experience and years at Alice James Books added polish to the final manuscript.

83

Enduring thanks to those poets who blurbed *Night Ladder,* the gifted and giving Brian Turner, the life-changing poetry of Joseph Fasano which informed several later poems in this book, and to Mary Kay Rummel whose own work harnesses the power of the sacred and helped me find the way.

To all friends who've offered support, Alice Pero, who pushed me out of the nest to share my first poem with an audience, soul sister Tina Halvorson, Susan Dobay – artist and fellow philosopher, Tamir Hendelman – jazz pianist extraordinaire, George Jisho Robertson – a most uncommon rose, the Faraway Poets – Ron Starbuck, Ambika Talwar, Jen Greenlea, Peter Shefler and Lin Ostler. To Diane Frank who is a whirling dervish of support and inspiration and finally to publisher Ami Kaye whose belief and encouragement sustained me through the perils of poetry and of life. You have my respect, honor and abiding trust. My great thanks to Steve Asmussen for all his work within and without *Night Ladder's* pages and to all the Glass Lyre staff who have helped shaped this book and bring it into being.

# ADDITIONAL PRAISE FOR *NIGHT LADDER*

In "Splendor" Lois P. Jones describes... What the photographer captured / when she slipped the lens / inside the cello to reveal / the prayer that burns inside/ every instrument / and you stood in its teak room / awash in the cleft of light... This astounding image encapsulates how poem after poem takes the reader of *Night Ladder* to the brink of the mystical and mundane, a visioning from the inside through a synesthetic response to paintings, music, places, history, love and desire. In refusing to deny the presence of the sacred in a life, maybe especially a secular life, she shows us how transformation waits at the edges of the simplest experiences. All of this and a pitch perfect ear make this book a necessary, inspiring, and beautiful guide to mindfulness. I would follow Lois P. Jones wherever her poems lead.

—**Mary Kay Rummel,** author of *The Lifeline Trembles*
and *Cypher Garden*

# ABOUT THE AUTHOR

**Lois P. Jones** is a recipient of the 2016 Bristol Poetry Prize, 2012 Tiferet Poetry Prize and the 2012 Liakoura Prize and was shortlisted for the 2016 Bridport Prize in poetry. Her poetry has been published in anthologies including *The Poet's Quest for God* (Eyewear Publishing), *Wide Awake: Poetry of Los Angeles and Beyond* (The Pacific Coast Poetry Series), *30 Days* (Tupelo Press) and *Good-Bye Mexico* (Texas Review Press). She has work published or forthcoming in *Tinderbox Poetry Journal, Narrative, American Poetry Journal, Tupelo Quarterly, The Warwick Review, Cider Press Review* and others. She is Poetry Editor of *Kyoto Journal,* host of KPFK's *Poets Café* (Pacifica Radio) and co-hosts Moonday Poetry. Lois's poems have won honors under judges Fiona Sampson, Kwame Dawes, Ruth Ellen Kocher and others.

# Glass Lyre Press

## exceptional works to replenish the spirit

Glass Lyre Press is an independent literary publisher interested in technically accomplished, stylistically distinct, and original work. Glass Lyre seeks diverse writers that possess a dynamic aesthetic and an ability to emotionally and intellectually engage a wide audience of readers.

Glass Lyre's vision is to connect the world through language and art. We hope to expand the scope of poetry and short fiction for the general reader through exceptionally well-written books, which evoke emotion, provide insight, and resonate with the human spirit.

Poetry Collections
Poetry Chapbooks
Select Short & Flash Fiction
Anthologies

**www.GlassLyrePress.com**